To Nicola, wishing you a very Happy Birthday with Lots of Love from
Auntie Sue, Uncle John, Brodie + Kenna X
X X X X X X X
1985

Published 1985 by
Les Éditions de l'Agora - SA - Genève
In association with
Hamlyn Publishing,
a division of The Hamlyn Publishing Group Limited,
Bridge House, London Road,
Twickenham, Middlesex, England

ISBN 600 30989 4

Printed in Switzerland

Mr GRUMPY'S BELONGINGS

Pascal MASSONNAT

HAMLYN

Once there was a fussy old man called Mr Grumpy. He liked everything to be just so — and if it wasn't — well, he could get very cross. One evening he came home in a very bad temper, and he was soon in a worse one. He switched on the light, and it didn't work. He looked for his slippers, but he couldn't find them anywhere.

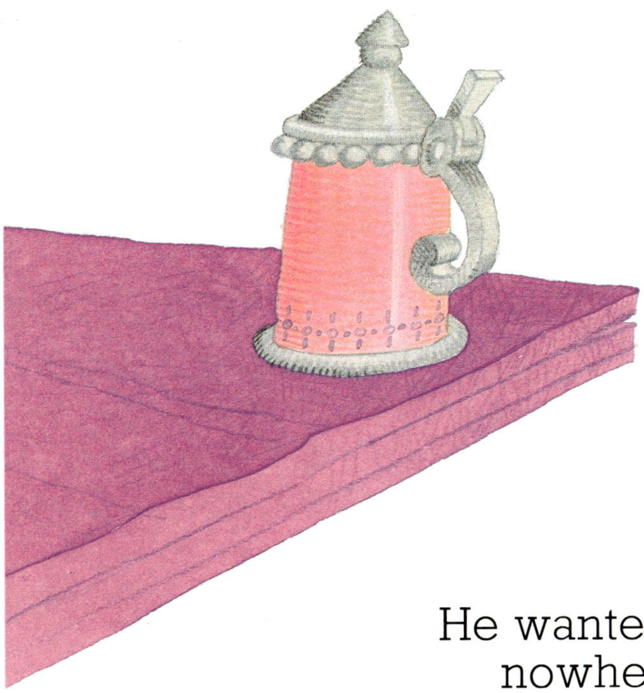

He wanted to smoke his pipe — it was nowhere to be seen. 'Grrr ...' he grumbled. 'I've just about had enough. I'm going to get rid of all these bits and pieces. None of them are any good.' And, mumbling to himself, he went off to bed.

That night, when Mr Grumpy was sound asleep, some very strange things began to happen.

A little man, who'd been standing there, quite still, all day, jumped out of the picture on the wall. He sat on the dresser. 'All right, everyone!' he called. 'Let's have a meeting!' Bonzo the dog could hardly believe his eyes! Everything came alive!

The desk lamp shone brightly, and the pipe began to cough. The pots and pans, the dusty old dictionary and all the little spice pots were chattering away.

'Now!' called the man from the painting. 'I'm calling this meeting to order. The situation is serious.'

'Yes it is,' muttered the spice pots. 'He wants to throw us out.'

'We can't let it happen,' said the table lamp. 'We'll just have to be kinder to him. If we all work properly, he'll realize how much he needs us.'

'We agree,' murmured the rest of the belongings, and they all shuffled off to their proper places.

Next morning, Mr Grumpy was
in a much better mood. He jumped
out of bed, put on his slippers
(they were in exactly the right place)
and went downstairs.

He enjoyed his breakfast. His egg was boiled just right, and for once the salt cellar wasn't blocked. His pipe was clean and no trouble to light.

'What a lovely morning!' he said to himself. 'Everything is just so!'

He went out that day in the best mood
he'd been in for weeks. He forgot all
about his plan to throw out
his belongings.

But Bonzo the dog wasn't at all happy. He'd hoped that if Mr Grumpy threw out all his belongings, he might spend a lot more time taking his faithful dog out for walks! But with everything behaving itself so well, there was no chance of Mr Grumpy doing anything of the kind.

So Bonzo spent all day making sure that NOTHING was in the right place, and that NOTHING would work properly. He hid the pipe under the armchair, and he took the slippers to the bottom of the garden. He licked all over the top of the salt cellar so that it would get completely blocked up.

The belongings couldn't do anything to stop him for they only came to life at night.

That evening, when Mr Grumpy came home, he was soon in a really bad temper!

His slippers had vanished. So had his pipe. And the chips he had for dinner were completely tasteless because he just couldn't get any salt out of the salt cellar.

'That's it!' he shouted. 'I've just about had enough. I need a break. I'm off to my auntie's, and when I get back, I'm going to get rid of everything. EVERYTHING!'

Next morning, still in a very bad temper, Mr Grumpy went off to stay with his auntie. He left Bonzo behind.

'Be good,' he told the dog. 'There's plenty of food and water for you. Just make sure you don't let any burglars in.'

And off he went.

That night, the belongings had an emergency meeting, and made a plan ...

The first thing they had to do was get rid of the dog. They shut him in the cellar — with his food and water of course!

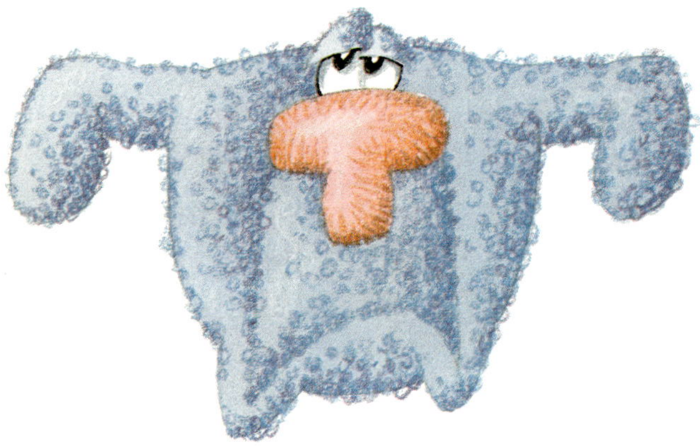

And then they all piled into the wheel-barrow and off they went to an empty house just down the road.

They made themselves comfortable and settled down to wait until Mr Grumpy came home. He'd soon see how much he needed them all!

Poor Mr Grumpy! Imagine how he felt when he opened his front door and saw that his house was almost completely bare. All his belongings had disappeared!

'I've been robbed!' he shouted.

In a panic, he ran through the house to see what had gone. He found poor Bonzo in the cellar.

'What sort of watch-dog are you?' he shouted. 'You've let them take everything!'

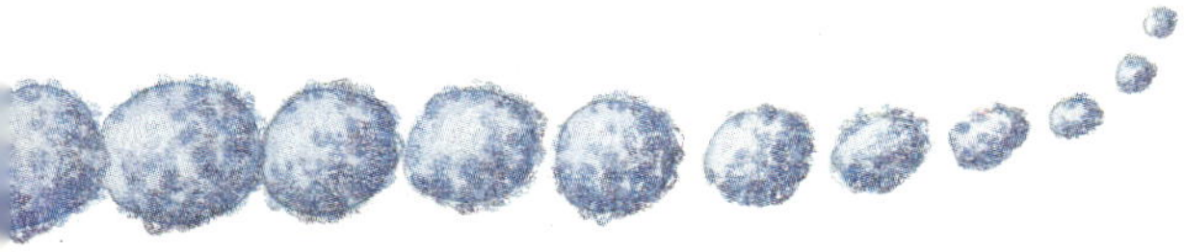

Mr Grumpy was miserable. How he missed his belongings! His comfortable slippers, his friendly old pipe, the desk lamp with its soft light, the funny picture at the top of the stairs … Oh! He did want them all back again.

He sat in an armchair under the bright standard lamp (one of the few things that hadn't gone) and tried to relax. It was impossible. He wasn't even cross any more. He was just dreadfully unhappy.

He knew now how very fond of
his belongings he was. He
thought about them all the time.

The next day, to cheer himself up, he took Bonzo for a walk. They went past an old, empty house ... and Bonzo smelled a familiar smell.

'That's funny,' he thought. 'I'm sure that's the smell of Mr Grumpy's pipe ... and his slippers! It's coming from that house ...'

Bonzo led his master up the path to the house and Mr Grumpy opened the door. He could hardly believe his eyes! There were all his missing belongings!

'Oh Bonzo!' he cried. 'You're a wonderful dog! You're so clever! You've found the burglar's hide-out. Congratulations! Let me shake your paw.'

In no time, the belongings were all back in their proper places, just so, the way Mr Grumpy liked them.

But of course, they didn't always stay that way and now and again the slippers would vanish or the pipe wouldn't light ... and of course Mr Grumpy was cross. But he tried to smile about it — for after all, he thought, he was lucky to have so many nice belongings.

And the belongings were happy too. They were glad to be home, and to celebrate they had a party — and they even invited Bonzo.

So! Be careful. Don't get too fussy and difficult to please ... you never know what might happen!